W9-ARY-358

THE SIMPLE GUIDE TO
CUSTOMS AND ETIQUETTE
IN
INDIA

COVER ILLUSTRATION

FRONT COVER: The seventeenth-century Taj Mahal in Agra
(in the northern state of Uttar Pradesh), considered by many to
be the most beautiful building in the world.
BACK COVER: The Raj Path, New Delhi

ABOUT THE AUTHOR

VENIKA KINGSLAND was born and grew up in India. She
was the co-founder of the Centre for Human Communication
in England, and later, the USA. She is a Registered Marketer
and now researches marketing on the Internet. She is the
author and co-author of a number of publications including
Complete Hatha Yoga and Hathapradipika.

Bicycle rickshaw

ILLUSTRATED BY
IRENE SANDERSON

THE SIMPLE GUIDE TO CUSTOMS AND ETIQUETTE IN

INDIA

VENIKA KINGSLAND

GLOBAL BOOKS LTD

Simple Guides • Series 1
CUSTOMS & ETIQUETTE

The Simple Guide to
CUSTOMS & ETIQUETTE IN INDIA
by Venika Kingsland

First published in 1996 by
GLOBAL BOOKS LTD
P.O. Box 219, Folkestone, Kent, England CT20 3LZ

ISBN 1–86034–050–4

British Library Cataloguing in Publication Data
A CIP catalogue entry for this book
is available from the British Library

Distributed in the USA & Canada by:
The Talman Co. Inc
131 Spring Street
New York, NY 10012
USA

Set in Futura 11 on 12 pt by Bookman, Slough
Printed in Great Britain by
The Cromwell Press Ltd., Broughton Gifford, Wiltshire

Contents

Indian Monsoon

Foreword

'Land of contrasts'

'India is a land of contrasts, of some very rich and many very poor people, of modernism and medievalism. . .India is not a poor country. She is abundantly supplied with everything that makes a country rich, yet her people are very poor. These words sound almost truer today than when Nehru penned them in jail in 1944. This is despite the progress that has been made in the face of a population that has more than doubled since India became independent. The teeming, overcrowded cities that never seem to sleep is the first thing that strikes the visitor on their first visit to India.

This vast continent is full of complexity and evident contradictions which are strong and sometimes provocative. India has great natural beauty and all the urban ugliness that is wrought by extreme poverty. Begging is a fact of life in India and something a visitor has to come to terms with. The truth is that India has had several good harvests and no one is really starving, certainly not in the villages where the majority of the population lives. In cities and the major tourist centres, begging is often a racket and organized in gangs, with the organizer taking the major share. But it is hard to resist the appeals of a small child and so it is better to give food. If, however, you must give money be discreet, as a crowd can soon gather.

Visit India and you will never be the same again say the tour operators and it is true; it is impossible to be unmoved. India will change you. Its very name stirs up the imagination and every visit to India is an adventure.

The contradiction of modern India can be understood by recognizing that it exists in several centuries at the same time. There is a small sophisticated modern society of a few million who live surrounded by hundreds of millions of primitive people. It has the largest pool of scientists and technologists after the USA yet over half of its population is illiterate.

It is difficult to generalize about India with its multi-layered culture of peoples, diversity of languages, attitudes and way of life. Yet from all this emerges a fundamental underlying cultural unity which gives rise to a distinctive way of being. I have no doubt that a basic awareness of the background, customs and way of life of what was once the 'Jewel in the Crown' of British colonial rule and is now described as a giant awakening will enable you to have a more rewarding visit.

V.M.K.

1

Land & People

'A huge, diverse country'

The Republic of India (Bharat) constitutes much of the greater portion of the Indian subcontinent. The term subcontinent is perhaps its most essential feature as its geographical characteristics have helped India maintain its isolation from the rest of Asia. It is rimmed by the Himalayan and lesser mountains on the north extending 2,000 miles into the Indian ocean in the south. It is bounded by Pakistan and the Arabian Sea on the west and Bangladesh, Myanmar (Burma) and the Bay of Bengal on the east. The distance between the oil-fields and tea-gardens in Assam and the Gujarati plains is 1700 miles. A huge country, 1,269,340 square miles, it is as large as Europe and even more diverse.

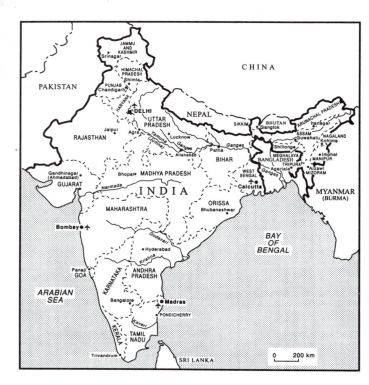

BRIEF HISTORY

A brief introduction to India's history will provide an insight into India's complex society. This distinctive culture has arisen through absorbing the numerous waves of migrating people who have been sweeping into India for several thousand years.

The highly civilized Harrappa Culture was well established around 2500 BC in the Indus valley, in the north-west of India. Five of the six major ethnic groups which make up the population of India today were already entrenched when the Aryans arrived around 1500 BC from Central Asia. The Aryans brought with them the four Vedas*, which are ancient Sanskrit hymns and devotional formulae. These have been preserved by the Hindu tradition - first orally and then written.

The word Aryan is somewhat contentious, but is correctly applied to this Indo-European group. The terms 'Hindu' and 'Hinduism' were coined by nations outside of India to designate the people and religion of the country to the east of the river Sindhu or Indus. Ironically, the river Indus after which India is named, is now in Pakistan.

The ancient Indians made notable intellectual contributions and laid the foundations for geometry, arithmetic and algebra. The zero and the decimal system reached Europe via the Arabs, hence the Arabic numerals.

Alexander the Great was so impressed by the high quality of the indigenous Ayurvedic medicine that he took physicians and practitioners back with him. This later returned to India as Unani - Greco-Arabian - medicine, with the Muslims and still flourishes side by side with Ayurvedic and modern Western medicine.

Around the 5th century the Huns, Turks and Mongols began coming in via Afghanistan and sowed seeds of disruption, some of which is evident even today.

The gospel of Christianity was spread by St Thomas – one of the original apostles – who was buried in Madras when he died. The 'incorrupt body' of St Francis Xavier is kept in a glass coffin in Goa and is brought out every ten years drawing Christians from all over the world.

In 1018 the Muslim rulers broke the power of the Hindu states making it easy for the

---

* Veda is a Sanskrit word meaning 'knowledge'.

The Governor of Bombay during the British Raj

Europeans to come in. The Portuguese came to Goa in 1497 and stayed until 1961; as one would expect, the five centuries of Portuguese influence has made it very different from the other states.

The English arrived in India when Queen Elizabeth I gave a charter to the East India Company in 1600. The foundation of Calcutta was laid by the British in 1690, who greatly influenced the present infrastructure. The British Raj came to an end in 1947 when India gained her independence, but left a lasting influence. It is said that the Victorian era is still alive and well in India.

THE PEOPLE

Statistics released by the Ministry of External Affairs suggest that the Indian population is 910 million (in reality probably over a billion) and growing at an annual rate of 2.5% despite extensive birth-control programmes. Yearly migration towards cities like Delhi is around 200,000. Around 70% of Indians live in the rural areas.

There are roughly three hundred million middle-class consumers with near European spending power. About the same number live, or try to live, below any humanly accepted poverty datum-line, and the rest get by somehow. A tiny proportion has phenomenal wealth and many of them belong to the Princely classes. Even at the height of the British Raj only three-fifths of India was under British rule. More than half a million square miles were fairly autonomous states under the rule of *Maharajas* – great kings, and *Nawabs* – Muslim ruling princes.

After their privy purses were abolished by Indira Gandhi whilst she was Prime Minister, some went into business and turned their Palaces into hotels. The Lake Palace Hotel at Udaipiur, made famous in the James Bond film *Octopussy*, is a good example.

There are more than a hundred different ethnic sub-groups within the country and yet India has remained a cohesive democracy since independence in 1947.

India is a secular state consisting of Hindus (83 per cent), Muslims (11 per cent), Christians (2 per cent), Sikhs (2 per cent), Buddhists, Jains, Parsees and B'hais amongst others. All religions have equal status but the sheer numbers of Hindus, make it the dominant religion.[1] This book, therefore, is biased towards the customs of the Hindus, although a mention of customs relating to other groups has been made wherever appropriate.

---

[1] Although Indians have learnt to live in harmony for most of the time, religious/communal riots do break out from time to time. The rise of Hindu fundamentalism in recent years has increased the problems between the Hindus and Muslims. Kashmir, (best avoided these days) has had a history of unrest because it has mostly had Hindu rulers and a Muslim population.

2

The Religions

Haruman, the monkey god

HINDUISM

Hinduism is a major world religion, not merely by virtue of its many followers (estimated at more than 800 million) but also because of its profound influence on various other religions during its long, unbroken history. It is also characterized by not having a founder.[2]

Hinduism has an extraordinary tendency to absorb foreign elements that have contributed to the religion's syncretism – the wide variety of beliefs and practices that it encompasses. As no one can *become* a Hindu, except by birth, incorporating other, older religions was perhaps the practical solution to increasing the numbers of Hindus.

Hinduism has many apparently contradictory forms including external observances and their rejection, extreme polytheism and high monotheism, animal worship, animal sacrifice and the refusal to take any form of life.

Interestingly enough, Hinduism is a convenient term for the religious beliefs and practices of the Hindus, and a term not generally used by them. They call it *Sanatana dharma* – the eternal way of life, and distinguish it from *Brahmanism*[3] or *Vedic Dharma*, which is essentially monotheistic, and that part of the religion that has come from the early Indo-European times.[4]

Modern Hinduism, as practised today, probably only goes back a thousand years. It was actively promoted at the time, presumably to stem the popularity of other religions such as Buddhism, Islam and Christianity.

The classical divisions in the Hindu system are:

> Vedas and the Upanishads:
> Ramayana, Mahabharat, Gita and Puranas
> Buddhistic and Jain period.

---

[2] See the forthcoming *A Simple Guide to Hinduism* by the same author for a more comprehensive description of the subject.

[3] The word Brahmanism pertains to Brahman – the absolute entity which is the ultimate reality in Hinduism, and should not be confused with Brahmin – a man of the Brahmin caste, one of the four hereditary castes, or Brahma, one of the Hindu triad.

[4] Bad translations of the Vedas have given a distorted and unfortunate view of the world. The Vedas were composed in a language similar to old Persian. They predate the Indo-European venture into the Indian subcontinent. The Vedic home is further North where sunlight and fire were greatly valued. In it society is sustained by high ethics and culture. Science is a central concern and technology is pursued. These were the people that produced the iron age. The Hittites retained these qualities and the earliest references to the Vedic gods were found in their inscriptions.

The two major epics which dominate are:

Ramayana – Composed by the poet Valmiki, its surviving text runs to 24,000 couplets celebrating the birth, education and adventures of Rama, the ideal man and king and his ideal wife Sita.

Mahabharat – The Great Epic of the Bharata Dynasty. This vast work of early Indian literature, running to 100,000 couplets, (seven times as long as *The Odyssey* and *The Iliad* combined), relates the struggle between two families, the Kauravas and the Pandavas. It also incorporates a mass of other romantic, legendary, philosophic and religious material from the heroic days of early Hinduism. Traditionally ascribed to the sage Vyasa it was probably the result of 2000 years of shaping before it reached its present written form circa AD 500. Included in it is the discourse between Krishna and Arjuna, the *Bhagwad Gita* – The Lord's Song, probably Hinduism's most important single text.

The televised version of these two epics, eighty or ninety episodes each, was viewed by over a 100 million viewers irrespective of religion.

THE CASTES

One of the most talked about and least understood elements of traditional Indian society is caste. The first three classes (*Brahmin*, or priestly; *Kshastrya*, or warrior; and *Vaishya*, or general populace – agricultural workers and artisans, and now include traders and money-lenders) are said to have been derived from the tripartite division of ancient Indo-European society, as evidenced in Greece and Rome. The *Shudras*, or servants were later added

Five-headed Brahma riding on a goose

when the Indo-Europeans settled into the Punjab and began to move down into the Ganges Valley.

The fifth group, roughly fifteen per cent of the population, consists of the outcasts or untouchables who do all the dirty jobs. The politically-correct term for them is Scheduled Castes, although Mahatma Gandhi gave them the name of *Harijan* – God's people.

Finally, the *Hijras*, who are distinguished by their distinctive style of dressing. There are almost a million of them living in organized groups all over India. The only non-heredity group, they comprise transsexuals, asexuals, transvestites, eunuches etc. Superstitious villa-

Rural village life

gers give any sexually-deviant children away to these groups, or an untouchable who has been castrated for urinating in front of a Brahmin might join them. They have been described in both the *Ramayana* and the *Mahabharat* and eunuches were used to guard the women's quarters in the Moghul period. They come from every religion and caste and obtain their living by singing, dancing and making lewd jokes at weddings and other ceremonies such as the birth of a son. They are at once hated, feared and respected. To be cursed by a Hijra brings terrible bad luck, but their blessing could give you a much wanted son and heir!

The caste system has evolved over thousands of years as a powerful way of organizing and administering an enormous mass of people. Although, traditionally, the four castes are said to have been produced by Brahma from different parts of his body at the time when the Vedas were revealed to the Brahmins, it is not necessarily a religious phenomenon. As a part of Indian life the caste system has even penetrated the other communities; for example, one sometimes hears of Brahmin Catholics.

The notion of *dharma*, (the obligation to accept one's condition and perform the duties appropriate to it) and *karma* (quality of action) is intrinsic to the whole principle of caste. According to these religious beliefs, each person is reincarnated on earth according to past behaviours. At this time they have a chance to be born into another, higher caste, but only if they have been *dharmic* – obedient to the rules of their caste in their previous life on earth.

Karma thus discourages people from attempting to cross caste lines for social relations of any kind. In this way, no one can

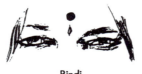

Bindi

escape from the cycle of dharma and karma, which has been pursued without envy if they are poor and without self-criticism if they are rich.

The belief that behaving in a dharmic way will bring about circumstances appropriate (favourable) to them, naturally gives people the licence to behave in any way they like. It enables them to ignore the plight of the poor and accept bribery and corruption as a way of life. This should provide an insight to those visitors who are often at a loss to understand how the extremes of wealth and poverty, animal worship and total animal neglect and abuse, can exist side by side.

Members of a higher caste often assume privileges like jumping to the top of the queue and expecting instant service in shops etc. They are mostly only recognized by the way they dress and their sense of superiority and attitude to others around them. Certain Brahmin priests have a recognizable *bindi* or *tilak* – markings on the forehead, depending on the temple or group they are attached to.

Applying the traditional *bindi* (a special red powder) to the forehead of both bride and groom is part of the Hindu marriage ceremony. The husband also applies *bindi* along the parting of the hair of his bride to signify that she is married. Today it has become a fashion item amongst young women, now that peel-and-stick bindies of every shade and hue are generally available!

The Hindus pray in temples – *mandirs*, which are found everywhere. Although the inner sanctums in many Hindu temples are off limits to non-Hindus, some temples will allow foreigners to go inside, but shoes must be left outside in every case. There is usually someone who will look after them for a couple of rupees.

Every October, the whole of city of Calcutta practically closes down for about ten days to celebrate Durga Puja. The Goddess Kali (another form of Durga or Parvati) is the main deity of the area. According to legend, when Siva's wife Parvati was cut up in pieces one of her fingers fell here. The actual temple was rebuilt in 1809 on a much older site. It is called Kalighat (which has been anglicized to Calcutta). The compound at Kalighat temple is usually blood-soaked from goats that have had their throats slit in order to appease her. Whole coconuts are also offered and smashed, often it is jokingly said, by the squeamish.

Another well known temple devoted to Kali is in Kamakhya, Assam, in Eastern India. It is a major centre for Tantric ritual where pigeons are sacrificed by the score. The practitioners of Tantra believe that the purpose of life is to embrace the whole of life itself. It is by responsible experimentation with life that the individual embraces reality as a whole rather than suffer from delusion fostered by partial knowledge.

Some animals, such as monkeys, snakes, bulls, elephants and eagles, are revered. Temples to Hanuman, the monkey god, are to be found in every city, town and Hindu village. Hanuman's wisdom and strength make him the patron god of Indian wrestlers. Long lines are to be seen in the morning and at lunchtime every Tuesday at one of the more famous temples in

New Delhi, as office workers come to say their prayers on Hanuman's day. It is therefore also considered auspicious to offer sweetmeats and fruits to monkeys as they wander in hordes near temples and the old parts of cities.

The temple of Karni Devi, together with her mount (a rat), is in Rajashtan near Bikaner. There are literally thousands of rats running everywhere and one has to be careful, because to tread on a rat can work out quite expensive. You are obliged to offer its weight in gold or silver if a white or black rat is hurt.

ISLAM

Islam, one of the world's most widespread religions is, with the exception of Sikhism, the newest of the world's great religions. Founded in Arabia in 622 AD, it is based on the teachings of Muhammad, who is called the Prophet. The Arabic word *islam* literally means 'to surrender', but as a religious term in the *Koran*, it means 'to surrender to the will or law of God'. One who practises Islam is a Muslim.

Taj Mahal, Agra

In mosques, where Muslims pray, shoes have to be removed as a mark of respect, but these can be carried under your arm.

SIKHISM

Influenced by the devotional emphasis of Hinduism and Sufi Islam, Sikhism is an ethical monotheism fusing elements of both religions. It was founded by Nanak, a mystic, who was born in 1469, and believed that God transcends religious distinctions. The followers of the Sikh religion are centred in Punjab State, in north-western India.

Sikh males are expected to join the Khalsa (Punjabi, 'pure'), a religious and military brotherhood. They must observe the five k's: the growing and retaining of *kes* – beard and hair, the wearing of *kacch* – soldiers' shorts, (both these are always to be prepared for war) *kirpan* – a steel dagger, *kanga* – a comb to keep neat and tidy and *kara* – an iron bangle to ward off evil.

Shoes are not allowed into Sikh temples – *gurudwaras*, and you are also required to cover your head before entering a temple.

Many Hindu and Jain temples do not allow any leather at all to be taken inside, such as belts, handbags, camera cases etc.

BUDDHISM

By the 6th century BC, Buddhism had begun to make its mark on India. It is the only religion to be founded by an Indo-European. It was founded by Gautama, the son of a rich Hindu *rajah* – king. After trying to find peace and a solution to the problem of universal suffering and misery through Hinduism and later Jainism, he experienced 'Enlightenment' at the age of 35. He preached that the only escape from suffering lay in complete renunciation and following the right path. This continued until his death at the age of 80. Buddhism, however, is better known outside India.

It is traditional to walk clockwise around Buddhist structures both inside and out. Do not smoke or drink alcoholic beverages on any hallowed ground, and be restrained when taking photographs.

JAINS

The Jains are members of a sect who are strict vegetarians and abhor violence so much that the orthodox amongst them even wear gauze masks so that they will not inhale and kill bacteria.

One of the most important tenets of Hinduism is *ahimsa*, the absence of a desire to injure, which is used to justify vegetarianism (although it does not prevent physical violence towards animals or humans, or blood sacrifices in temples).

There are many tribes living in the regions bordering Mynamar and Tibet who are more isolated from the mainstream of Indian life and still retain a vigorous and colourful culture of their own.

Sikh festival

3

Custom and Ritual

Kumbh Mela, Allahabad

The Indians love religious *melas* (fairs). The biggest of these – the Hindu Kumbh Mela – is billed as the largest religious festival in the world. It is suggested that as many as 27 million people wash away their sins in the holy rivers Ganges and Jamuna in Allahabad (Uttar Pradesh) on the main festive day. The elderly go to the Kumbh Mela in the hope of dying there, as it is believed that dying at the Kumbh will give them *moksh* – liberation from the cycle of birth and death. This is also considered true of the city of Varanasi, where it is not uncommon to have to step over dead bodies in the streets.

Amongst Hindus, rituals begin before birth and the first time the child eats solid food – usually rice. As the child grows older, rites include the first haircutting, where the hair is completely shaved off for a young boy, and purification after the first menstruation for a young girl.

Prayers are offered to Sarwasti the goddess of learning, before starting at school, then the sacred thread ceremony for adolescent boys of the first three castes and then comes marriage. This is followed by blessings upon a pregnancy, to produce a male child and to ensure a successful delivery and the child's survival of the first six dangerous days after birth.

Last are the funeral ceremonies – cremation and, if possible, the sprinkling of ashes in a holy river such as the Ganges. Ganges water is carried by Hindus around the world because it should be the last thing that is put into the mouth when a Hindu dies.

Hindus are generally cremated on open wooden pyres. The size of the pyre depends on the social status of the family. The funeral pyre constructed to cremate an ex President of India, – a Sikh, recently used four quintals of wood (400 kilos), some of it precious sandalwood. Seven tins (18 kilos each) of pure *ghee* (clarified butter) mixed with 30 kilos of *havan samagri* (herbs & spices used for Vedic ceremonies) were thrown on to flames whilst Brahmin priests chanted verses from the Vedas. All this to a 21-gun salute followed by the sounding of the Last Post.

Yearly offerings to dead ancestors include a mixture of rice and sesame seeds offered by the eldest male child so that the ghost of his father may pass from limbo into rebirth.

Muslims are generally buried; the Taj Mahal in Agra is a beautiful example of a mausoleum in the Indo-Islamic style. It was built in the seventeenth century of white marble inlaid with gemstones by the Mughal emperor Shah Jahan as a tomb for his cherished wife.

In Goa at Christian burials a slow band playing mournful music precedes the cortège whilst fire crackers are let off every now and again, probably to ward off the devils! The Parsis, who were originally refugees from Persia, deal with their dead by exposing them on high platforms (Towers of Silence) to be torn up and devoured by the vultures.

In daily ritual amongst the Hindus, generally the wife does *puja* (prayers). Statues of the gods (silver if you are well off and brass if you are not) are bathed and dressed. Offerings of fruit and flowers are then made to them in a small shrine in the house. The wife also makes offerings to local snakes or trees or obscure spirits (benevolent and malevolent) dwelling in her own garden or at crossroads or other magical places in the community. The men will do a similar *puja* before starting work.

MARRIAGE

In the days before people moved into towns, marriages were arranged amongst people you knew, or through the local barber or priest. Now amongst the middle classes, marriages are arranged through the auspices of classified advertisements in the Sunday papers. There are very few interreligious or intercast marriages and the advertisements are classified to reflect this. (See examples opposite.)

Indian wedding

Bachelor, US, resident, holder of Green Card, University qualified, Goan Catholic Brahmin, 29 years, 5′ 5″ tall, slim, light complexion, seeks educated, fair Catholic girl, preferably Brahmin, under 24 years, for marriage. Please reply with recent photo and personal details to Box. . .

Alliance invited for a Home-loving sober girl from middle-class, respected, Punjabi Sikh family. 26/4′10″ B.E.(Civil) Convent educated. Preferred Architect or Engineering field with equal status. Kindly reply with details to Box. . .

Hindus, Sikhs, Muslims and Christians are married by priests. Hindu marriages are generally performed at home by walking seven times around a ceremonial holy fire.

Indian weddings are spectacular theatrical events. The celebrations generally last at least three days and are preceded amongst the Hindus, by the bridegroom on a white charger and his entourage going to the bride's home accompanied by a brass band.

Child marriage, though illegal, still prevails in the villages. Occasionally, a two-year-old girl will be seen being carried around the holy fire on a tray by her father behind the bridegroom.

Legislation in recent years now gives a woman the same status as her male counterpart; in reality, though, women are still treated as second-class citizens and some organizations only pay lip-service to equal opportunities. But many women do go out to work.

It is also difficult for a woman to instigate divorce proceedings whatever the religion. Indeed, the late Prime Minister Rajiv Gandhi bowed to Muslim fundamentalist demands that Muslim women should not be subjected to civil laws concerning divorce. 'Saving face' and *izzat* – self respect – is all important and a man will go to great lengths, even bribing the court officials to delay the proceedings if the woman has asked for a divorce; in this way, he ensures that if a divorce is imminent it is he who should ask for it. Goan women are notably different, perhaps because the State of Goa has a law whereby the women are entitled to half the family property.

The attitude to a widow is that she must be a harbinger of bad luck which is why her husband died. The old women in the community describe the widow as 'the one who ate her husband'. Her glass bangles are smashed as soon as the husband dies and the *bindi* – the red mark on her forehead, which often denotes being married – is wiped off. In certain groups, the custom of shaving her head still continues.

In orthodox families she is not allowed anywhere near a newly-wed, nor is she welcomed at auspicious gatherings. It is no wonder that becoming *sati* – self immolation on the husband's funeral pyre – is considered an option in villages. However, once she has made up her mind the widow is treated as a goddess and hundreds of people visit the site of the pyre. Outlawed in the nineteenth century, the practice still continues.

Indians venerate the astrologers and are also very superstitious. Every village has its *pundit* – priest/astrologer. They are very important not only for weddings but are also consulted before the start of any business venture. Indians are obsessed with the notion that someone might cast an 'evil eye' or *nazar* on them and several things are done as a safeguard. Babies have a customary black spot placed behind their ears so that people will notice the black spot rather than the beauty of the child. Buildings under construction have a horrific face painted on a large pot or a demonic figure displayed on the front to scare away evil spirits. If someone does fall victim to *Nazar*, then there are many home-grown remedies, with prayers and various activities conducted by the local priest as a last resort.

Dowries have to be provided for daughters, irrespective of religion. Even the Christians do, as it is a matter of *izzat* or self-respect to show the rest of the community that you can provide for your daughter. Dowries are illegal,

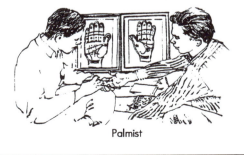

Palmist

nevertheless parents feel obliged to spend huge amounts of money and in some cases will take on large debts. It is all about 'saving face.' This is a subject not to be discussed.

India's own statistics show that a 'dowry death' takes place every hundred minutes. Ostensibly, greedy in-laws cause the death of new brides if they do not bring a sufficiently large dowry. The most common cause is said to be 'kitchen' death, with the unlikely story that somehow kerosene, which is one of the most common fuels for cooking, got splashed on the daughter-in-law and burnt her to death before anyone could get to her. Consequently, every couple wants to have a male child.

NATIONAL HOLIDAYS

Fixed dates for some national holidays are 26 January – Republic Day, 1 May – Labour Day, 15 August – Independence Day, 2 October – Mahatma Gandhi's Birthday, 25 December – Christmas Day. Festive days are proclaimed as public holidays depending on the dominant religion in the state. Dates vary according to the religious calendar, phases of the moon etc. and it is always useful to phone before visiting Government offices.

Local holidays include ones like *Poshi Punam* – when all little girls are taught to cook rice for the first time, usually *kheer* – rice pudding. By the time she is considered a woman she is expected to know at least fifteen different ways of preparing rice.

A word of caution: travelling anywhere on *Holi* – the Hindu festival of colour, usually celebrated in March – is definitely to be avoided as most Indians, regardless of religion, go crazy and drench everyone and everything in coloured water, coloured powder, paint and other unmentionable things. This is usually followed by offering friends sweets and a pleasant tasting concoction of milk and ground almonds, liberally laced with *bhang* (hashish) or beer.

For one month of the year, Ramadan, all Muslims fast during the hours of daylight. They do not eat or drink. They are tolerant of foreigners but it would put a great strain on them if they were invited to, say, a business lunch during this time. The end of this month is celebrated by a public holiday – *Id-ul-Fitr*.

Muharram is a ten-day Muslim festival commemorating the martyrdom of Mohammed's grandson, Imam Hussain.

There are several colourful events worth attending at different times of the year if you happen to be there:

Festival	Place	Time of the Year
Republic Day	New Delhi	26 January
Kite Festival	Ahmedabad	January
Desert Festival	Jaisalmer	Early February
Rath – Chariot Festival	Puri	June/July
Snake Boat Races	Allapuzha	August/ September
Dussehra – held for ten days, it is also called *Durga Puja* in Bengal.	Mysore Delhi Calcutta Kulu	September/ October
Diwali – festival of the lights	all around the country but particularly Delhi.	November
Camel Fair	Pushkar	November
Christmas	Goa	December

4

The Home

English-style bungalow

The British influence is evident in the bungalows in the cities. The middle classes also live in flats and high-rise apartments that could be anywhere in the world. Only the kitchens and bathrooms have their own characteristics.

Middle-class homes have a Western-style toilet but most others will have an Indian-style toilet where you place your feet on either side of a hole and then squat to go. In older parts of cities this facility can be shared by several buildings. Usually a hole in the ground, it might be two bricks on either side of a pit. In trains you can see the rail track through the hole! There is never any toilet paper as its use is repellent to most Indians. It is generally believed that a greater level of cleanliness is achieved by using water.

There is usually a tap by the side of the toilet and a small pot. Afterwards the business of cleansing takes the form of cold water being splashed by the left hand in the appropriate direction. It is understandable that nothing is accepted in the left hand as it is considered unclean and never used for eating with. In rural India, you will see the villagers heading for the fields at dawn with a small water pot. The hands are then cleaned with a little mud and water.

If your hosts are well travelled they may go out of their way to get some toilet paper in for you. Better hotels and restaurants will have adequate toilet facilities but a toilet roll and soap are essential items in your baggage, together with a universal sink plug as wash-hand basins never seem to have any.

Indians like to wash in running water; bathing in tub-water sullied by one's own dirt is considered repellent. The Westernized rich have at least one bath tub in the house.

Most Indians who can afford it take bucket baths. Bathrooms have a bathing area, a square which is about two inches below the rest of the room. There is usually a tap and a shower which never seems to work, as there is a water shortage in most Indian cities. The Indians fill up a bucket, crouch and pour the water over themselves using a mug.

Kitchens are quite primitive, and very rarely will have running hot water. The rich middle classes usually have a cook and one or two other servants. Although some orthodox families who adhere to strict dietary practices will not entrust the preparation of food to someone who is not of their caste or religion. A Brahmin cook is the exception as their cooking will be acceptable on religious feasts by other Brahmins. Even in homes where the housewife does her own cooking she will have a part-time servant who will come in to do the dishes.

It is customary to take your shoes off when entering a traditional home but not otherwise. In such situations it is sensitive to do as your host does, or in any case ask for their advice.

SOCIAL RELATIONS

Various communities have traditionally pursued carefully defined occupations. The Punjabis are considered to be excellent farmers, the Marwaris, a small, closely-knit community originally from the western state of Rajasthan, are industrialists and money-lenders. The Tamils from South India, bureaucrats, Gujaratis have been traders and merchants. The Jains had traditionally served as accountants to the Muslim rulers and now are good at money management. They also account for half the world's trade in small, polished diamonds.

In India everybody is labelled by their name. No more than a name is sufficient to put anybody in his or her place. And that place is never, as it is supposed to be in the West, designed for the personality of a single individual. It positions the individual in a specific community whose attributes are assumed in advance. So, for example, the family name of a Brahmin might be *Divedi* – this would mean they were from a community where two Vedas were studied. (If it was from a place where three Vedas were studied it would be *Trivedi*, or four Vedas it would be *Chaturvedi*.)

Certain South Indian groups have a very intricate naming system. Take, for example, someone called R.V. Ramamurthy. Ramamurthy will be the personal name, and the

Family behaviour on the beach

initials will denote the name of the ancestral village and the father. Certain Parsees have a peculiar system and derive their names from their occupation, for example, Mr Doctor or Mr Mistry (mechanic) or Mr Bottleopenerwallah – *wallah* – person who is or does, therefore 'one who opens bottles.'

In traditional homes there is a formal institutionalized code of conduct for various categories of family members towards various other categories. Everyone knows their place and how to behave. People rarely say please or thank you, as there is no need. This is also carried into the workplace apart from the airlines, which is the only place you are likely to hear it. Everything is prescribed, from the way the young members of the family greet the elders – such as whose feet must be touched in the morning and in which order, to how many saris and cooking utensils are to be included in the dowry. The eldest married lady of the house reigns supreme and rules over her sister/daughter-in-laws with a rod of iron.

Relationships are evident from the names of various relationships – for example, *Dada* – Paternal grandfather, *Dadi* – paternal grandmother, *Nana* – maternal grandfather, *Nani* – maternal grandmother, *Chacha* – father's younger brother, *Chachi* – his wife; *Taya* – father's older brother, *Tayi* – his wife. *Devar* – husband's younger brother, *Devarani* – his wife.

The Indian form of Mr & Mrs is Shri and Shrimati (abbreviated to Smt.). Sikh men will have the word Singh (lion) and Sikh women have Kaur (princess) after their personal name followed by the family name e.g. Sher Singh Aluwalia or Gurmeet Kaur Saund. Muslim men will often refer to their wife as *Begum* – a Muslim woman of high rank.

In general, the polite form of address *Aap* – 'thou', is reserved for the elders, seniors or upper castes. Servants and children are addressed as *Tum* – 'you'. Attaching 'Ji' to any name, is to show respect. For example, *Masterji, Bhai* (brother)*ji, Memsahibji* (this left-over from the old Raj days, refers to the lady of the house).

Under no circumstances will an Indian wife say her husband's name aloud as it is considered to be disrespectful. When addressing him she will use all manner of oblique references – such as '*ji*' or 'look here' or 'hello' or in some extreme cases refer to her husband as the father of her child!

Body Language – nodding the head up and down is clearly a 'yes', and shaking the head from side to side is a 'no'. However, the most common gesture is a funny rotational movement of the head. This is very character-istic of the Indians and can have several meanings. With a smile it might be – 'OK – I understand', or it could be 'maybe' more often than not it is 'I couldn't care less!'

The Indians as a group are warm, hospitable people and take every opportunity to be friendly to foreigners, sometimes uncomfortably so. They will insist on offering you food and drink even if you do not want it. The best policy if you really do not want what is being offered is to politely and firmly say 'no' with a smile and explain that you have just eaten. Quite often even total strangers on meeting you will ask you to visit them at their home, they will persist until you agree, but no one will be more surprised if you take them at face value and turn up. In such circumstances it is best to respond with: 'Oh yes one day we will visit you.' You are then expected to forget all about it. If you really wish to take up the offer then it is wise to clarify and arrange a firm date and time.

GREETINGS

Indians generally greet each other and say goodbye with palms held together as if saying prayers, and say *Namaste* – which literally means – 'I recognize the self in you'. For Hindi speakers this is usually followed by *Kya hal hai?* ('how is your health?'); *teak taak* ('all right') in both cases the 't' is aspirated. *Teak hai* or *Achha* ('OK') is used for everything from answering a general enquiry to an affirmation that the road is clear.

'Namaste'

Muslims use the well-known *salaam aleikum* – 'peace be upon you' – the reply being *aleikum assalaam* – 'and on you peace'. If in doubt it is quite safe to just say 'hello' with a smile.

PRESENTS

There is no tradition of taking presents if you are invited to visit an Indian family, but anything European or American is always appreciated, particularly cosmetics for the ladies. The very best gift you can take your business partner is a bottle of Scotch whisky, although it may not be welcome if they are Muslims. If you are staying with an Indian family then it is appropriate to invite them out for a meal to a good restaurant.

TABOO SUBJECTS

Bodily contact, even the simplest hug or kiss, between men and women is considered provocative and likely to invite rough treatment in most of India. Goans who are more Latin-American in their outlook are the exception. Although even in Goa discretion is advised, as Goa is also popular with visitors from other Indian states.

India is quite conservative in its dress and the amount of harassment received by a Western woman is directly related to the amount of flesh exposed. Plunging necklines and strapless tops will invite remarks and stares. Knee-length skirts and trousers are fine. Travelling in certain parts such as Muslim areas calls for even more restraint. Women might consider adopting the popular *Salwar* and *Kameez*, the local baggy long trousers and shirt. These are very comfortable and inexpensive, and available ready-made in all sizes in beautiful materials and designs.

It is not socially acceptable for Indian women to be touched by any male other than husband or child, and then by the husband only in private. So only shake hands with an Indian woman if she offers it first. This goes for Western-style dancing as well. If you are invited to a disco or restaurant it is as well to check with your host what the local custom is.

You often see men holding hands and occasionally, much to the indignation of a Western male, they will persist in holding his hand just to affiliate.

The left hand is considered unclean and so taking or eating anything with the left hand should be avoided.

Sex, together with homosexuality and lesbianism, is not a subject that is discussed openly, although plenty goes on. Typically in parties, the women sit on their own drinking Coca Cola and discussing the latest film or the problem with servants, whilst the men drink whisky and crack schoolboy jokes with sexual overtones.

SENSE OF HUMOUR

It is not easy for the Indians to laugh at themselves as they take themselves very seriously. They have an unsophisticated sense of humour and only a tiny portion would enjoy black humour. On the whole, they enjoy slapstick and will laugh merrily at someone else's misfortune, like slipping up on a banana skin. Traditionalists hate the idea of caricatures of people they respect, although it is increasingly fashionable to make jibes at the politicians.

5

City Life

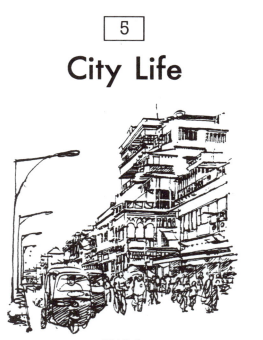

Old Delhi

About 30% of the population live in cities. These are Delhi – the capital, Bombay the largest city with over nine million, Calcutta and Madras. Other cities with a population of more than one million include Hyderabad, famous for its handicrafts; Bangalore, the silicon capital; Ahmadabad with its sumptuous brocades; Pune; the leather manufacturing city of Kanpur; Lucknow; Nagpur; Surat in Gujrat – famous for its silk prints; Jaipur, called the pink city, after the colour of the stone used to build the palaces; Indore; Coimbatore; Vadodra; Patna; Madurai; Bhopal, made famous by the Union Carbide disaster; and the holy city of Varanasi, so called because of its many temples and location on the banks of the sacred Ganges River.

INDIAN DANCING

Visitors should make every effort to see a performance of classical dancing (usually to be found in any of the larger cities) – one of the most highly developed arts of Indian culture. It was an integral part of Sanskrit dramas, a mode of worship performed in the inner shrines of every temple, and a courtly pastime.

The four principal schools of Indian dance, as they are now designated, are *bharata natyam*, *kathakali* – the dance dramas of the Kerala region, *kathak* – a dance style of the north of India, where the powerful Mughal dynasty ruled, and *manipuri*, the fourth major school, originated in the northeastern state of Manipur, where Hindus fled from Muslim persecution. The dancing, which has remained remarkably free of outside influence, is noted for its graceful turning and swaying.

Of these, *bharata natyam* is significant in being one of the most complete dance sciences in existence. It is based on the principles set down in the *Natya Shastra* – science of dance – a handbook on dramaturgy that was supposedly written about AD 200 by a Hindu sage, Bharata, according to instructions from the god Brahma.

Indian dancing

'OPEN' SOCIETY

Unlike many other Third World countries, India is an open society where locals and foreigners can generally move about freely. Foreign correspondents will tell you that they are not followed around by men in cars as happens in certain other developing countries which do not share India's commitment to democratic values and human rights. The Indian Government does not censor transmissions to outside news agencies and the Internet is gaining momentum.

However, caution should be exercised with regards to moving about after dark as one would in many of the major cities of the world.

As a corollary to the subject of sex not being openly discussed, there are strong social forces which prevent the kind of intermixing of men and women that is normal in Western countries. This results in the majority of single and married adult males using prostitutes in many areas.

If you are a male travelling alone you may well be invited to experience this aspect of city life. The cages of Bombay are famous. This is a whole street where prostitutes are on show behind bars. However, the social taboo on openness about these matters has meant there has been an ineffectual response to the problem of AIDS which is becoming quite serious.

Eve Teasing – the sexual harassment of young woman – has reached epidemic proportions and is regularly reported in the newspapers. With the advent of satellite television, together with the restrictions of traditional Indian society this problem is growing. White women particularly are viewed as easy targets.

CINEMA

Films play a tremendously important role in everyday life. Indians are obsessed by film-stars and hold them in very high esteem. A popular film-star going in for politics can be assured of instant success. India turns out over a thousand films a year but television is now emerging as the public's favourite medium. The Indian film industry affectionately known as 'Bollywood' is the largest in the world purely in volume terms. The majority of films are produced to a *masala* – 'mixed spice' – formula with three vital ingredients: music, violence and romance. Although most of it is cheap escapism for the masses, some superb directors have emerged. Foremost among them was Satyajit Ray who gained international recognition with *Pather Panjali*.

Recently, Indian film censors allowed kissing scenes to be shown in Indian films, scenes that were previously only seen in foreign movies. Nudity is still prohibited and it is no wonder that there is a healthy black market in videos. Everything North American is coveted, *Dynasty* and *Dallas* are the role models the Indian elite looks to. The teenagers worship *Baywatch* and the whole family sits down for *The Bold and the Beautiful*.

Family feast: *'The Bold and the Beautiful'*

6

Food & Drink

A feast of Indian food

Indians love eating out and in the main city centres the range of eating places is very wide, with every kind of food available – from expensive Western-style and Chinese restaurants to little stalls selling *chaat* – a fiery mixture of fruit and vegetables. But do remember, if there is a choice it is important to stress that there should be no chillies in the food. Your phrase book will tell you that *garam* is hot, but that is referring to temperature. Many foreigners ask for food that is not *garam* and end up with cold fiery hot food!

TEA

India is the world's largest tea producer and in common with Britain, tea is its number one beverage. British associations with Indian tea go back to 1662 when Queen Catherine, wife of Charles II, introduced tea-drinking to the English as a social habit when she brought chests full of tea as part of her dowry.

Little did Mrs Harris, the wife of the House-keeper and Beadle of the East India Company realize that she was starting such a significant 'corporate' tradition by making *chai* – tea – for the Directors of the Company at committee meetings in 1666 in Calcutta. This tradition was to last for more than 300 years and cause a national outcry when British companies decided to replace the traditional 'tea lady' with vending machines.

Chai is offered to you at all times and everywhere you go in India. The *Dhabas* – roadside restaurants – provide delicious cups of *Masala* tea or coffee, which is generally milky, sweet and flavoured with cardamoms.

The *Dhaba* is contrived with odd boards and sheets of galvanized iron, with wooden tables and benches. The food they serve is cooked on a brazier and is delicious if you can bear to share it with the flies.

DAILY DIET

Morning tea is between 6 and 7 am. Then depending on which part of India you are in, breakfast can be *mathis* (savoury fried biscuits) and *jalebis* (sticky syrupy fried sweets) in the North, *idli* and *sambar* (steamed rice cakes and lentils) or *dosas* – crispy rice pancakes, which are 24 inches in diameter, served with delicious hot coffee in the South. *Pau roti* – white bread is generally available. Restaurants will serve eggs in a number of ways. Single fried (sunny side up) or double fried, Rumble Tumble (scrambled) should be avoided as the eggs might be of questionable age and origin!

Lunch is between 1 and 2 pm, and consists of rice and curry. Dinner is usually served at about 8.30 pm. However, dining late, like serving Scotch whisky and French wines, is a status symbol.

When invited out, the meal is likely to be in a British-style club or a restaurant and the fare will be similar to that in the West. If you are invited to an Indian home, you will be expected to join in with the family and friends around the dining table, occasionally served buffet-style.

As a foreigner you might be offered a fork but most people will eat with their fingers. Remember never to eat with your left hand, and if asked to pass the salt, never place the salt in the hand of the person asking for it, it is considered bad luck. In traditional families the guests and men are served first with the women eating afterwards.

A complete meal will consist of six traditional items – *dal* – split lentils, rice, vegetable, yoghurt and chutney, *roti* or *chappati* (flat unleavened bread, generally not fried, other varieties include – *puri, paratha, naan*, the last two can also be baked in a *tandoor* – a kind of a deep oven with live coal). Chappaties made of freshly kneaded dough are rolled out thin and cooked on a hot *tawa* – a kind of griddle –

Betal palm leaves

and then toasted until puffed up on an open fire. The Hindus cook their chappaties on a convex *tawa* and the Muslims on a concave one.

The dessert is often fruit in custard, or *kheer* – rice pudding or some sticky sweets. In the summer months you will be served with *kulfi* and *faluda* – Indian ice-cream and sweet noodles flavoured with saffron and rose water – quite delicious!

You help yourself or are served with a small amount of the numerous dishes and some form of bread. A small piece of which is torn off and used to scoop up the vegetable or curry. The south Indians have made the eating of rice and *sambhar* – a regional concoction of lentils and vegetables – into a fine art. The rice and lentils are mixed into little balls and then dextrously popped into the mouth.

'Modern' Indians will serve soup as a first course at dinner. Dinner generally ends with '*paan*' a national obsession. *Paan* – *areca* (betel) nut, lime, spices and condiments are wrapped in fresh betel leaf, the whole of which is then placed in the mouth and chewed. It is considered to be a digestive. Stalls selling them are to be found everywhere, crammed into any available space and in front of restaurants. You can get designer *paans* –

sadda – plain, *mitha* – sweet or filled with your favourite chewing tobacco or cocaine, covered with gold or silver leaf. It is customary to serve the groom with a special *paan* on the wedding night. Aptly named – *Palang tor* – bed-breaker, it supposedly contains aphrodisiacs.

Be careful though if you decide to try a *paan* as the woody betel nut can be a *tooth-breaker* to Western teeth not used to them. When finished with chewing you can spit out the leftover juice to join the other orange stains that spatter corners, walls, and pavements everywhere.

Quite often, you will see a rope hanging on a hook at the *paan* stall with a lighted end so that customers can light their cigarette or *bidi* – (pronounced 'beerrie'). Bidis are small vile-smelling indigenous cigarettes that are wrapped in a cheap grade of tobacco leaf.

A large proportion of Hindus are vegetarians, a lavish meal is where one serves 33 different preparations of vegetables and 33 different Indian sweets. As meat is becoming increasingly popular in homes and the better restaurants it is safe, but pork is definitely to be avoided. Hindus who are not vegetarians do not eat beef, neither do the Sikhs. The Muslims do not eat pork as the pig is considered an unclean animal, nor are they supposed to drink alcohol.

WATER

When it comes to drinking water, DO NOT! is the rule unless you know it has been boiled *and* filtered. The same rule should apply to ice and the water used for brushing teeth. There is plenty of bottled mineral water avail-able, but check the cap of any bottled drink to make sure that it is the genuine article and has not been filled by someone around the corner.

Indians usually drink water with their meals. You may be offered *nimboo pani* – fresh old-fashioned lemonade or *Lassi* – a yoghurt drink; in both cases check that it has been made with cooled boiled water. Indian beer is excellent and so is the rum; gin is passable. Indian whisky is reasonable, at least at the top of the range, lethal at the bottom.

Pub culture is growing in the major cities like Bombay and Bangalore, but people generally drink in restaurants and clubs. In Goa which is different from any other state in India, there are several bars on every street. Excise duty is low, and excellent chilled lager-like beer is available at Rs 20 a litre in most bars, and three times that price in the 5-star hotels. The local *fenny* (somewhat like cheap *Eau d'vie*) is distilled both from coconut and the cashew apple. Beloved of the locals, you have to get a permit to take it out of the state. The other local drink is *Urak* – similar to the so-called – *snake juice* – both legally and illegally distilled all over India and stomach searing.

The restaurants and the *Shacks* – temporary huts that serve excellent food and drink on the beaches during the tourist season – generally remain open until midnight. Although there are a few that are open all night.

There is prohibition in certain States like Gujarat, Andhra Pradesh and recently Haryana, and it has inevitably spawned an illegal market in liquor. Indeed, in Ahmedabad a once nomadic tribe known as Charas distil a cheap liquor also known as *Charas* in the suburbs. Foreigners can get permits to drink in these states.

Indian sweets

Indian sweets are sticky confections, covered with real silver flakes and flavoured with cardamoms, nutmeg, saffron and other spices. The sweet stalls are a colourful extravaganza, with different varieties in different parts of India. Most Indian women love these sweets and often suffer from a high incidence of sugar diabetes.

TIPPING

In India you tip not so much for a good service but to get things done, more like the origin of the word 'tip' itself. In the London coffee houses of the 18th century, merchants would place money for waiters and the serving wenches in boxes marked T.I.P. 'To Insure Promptness.' Tipping is not necessary in the cheaper restaurants, family-run businesses and taxis. However, if you are going to visit an establishment frequently, a programme of unexpected and intermittent tips will ensure the standards are kept up.

SHOPPING

India assails all your senses. The exotic blaze of colours, the blasting heat and dust, the scents – fruits and vegetables – huge mounds of them – mangoes, watermelons, limes, ginger and yard-long squash. Flowers – jasmine and tuberoses, marigolds and roses, spices – great piles of turmeric, chillies, cinnamon and cardamom, sandalwood and of course incense everywhere.

Nowhere is this more obvious than in the markets in the old parts of cities, away from touristy areas. These are organized by commodities, so spices are sold in one street whilst clothes in another. There are entire streets that sell gold or silver jewellery, gemstones or pearls. Of all the decorative arts in India, jewellery is the most universally interesting and beautiful. Filigree work, which disappeared in Europe after the end of the Roman Empire and introduced again by the Moors in the 15th century, was never lost in India.

Fish and meat are not only sold in separate areas, meat is butchered in different ways to suit religious requirements. *Halal* (killed slowly according to Allah's laws) for the Muslim community and *jhataka* (swift) for the Hindus. Meat is displayed by hanging in open stalls decorated with countless flies. You can choose your own chicken from the poor birds in cages under the stall and have it killed in front of you to ensure freshness.

Almost everything can be obtained from *Chemists & General Stores*. From medicines and cosmetics to toilet rolls and Nescafé, different stores may specialize in different commodities.

Be alert when shopping, bargain hard and generally do not trust shopkeepers' descriptions of quality. Government handicraft emporiums have a fixed price and the quality is usually reliable. Every state has its own emporium.

7

Business

'. . .women are found at every level of business'

Since July 1991, India's economic isolation, which had been one of the cornerstones of her post-independent policy, has been replaced by liberalization and economic reforms. Impressive changes are being stimulated with many import restrictions abolished and tariff barriers being notably reduced. The rupee is fully convertible for purposes of trade and direct financial investment is now permitted. The financial industry has been deregulated as regards mutual funds.

Industrialists petitioning for new licences for expansion or for joint ventures with foreign partners are finding their applications being processed with greater ease. There is also no shortage of individuals and organizations claiming to have the knowledge and expertise to represent you in India. Western firms are now inundated by unsolicited letters from Indians wanting to become their agents. As some of them might be unscrupulous, it is worth researching them thoroughly. Quality control is new to India and occasionally there is a great difference in the samples shown to win an order and the goods that are eventually shipped.

There are 22 stock exchanges, and it is often stated – 7,000 quoted companies – of which perhaps just over a thousand are active, and over 25 million shareholders. Shares are available on every street corner in practically every kind of enterprise. Long queues can be seen at lunch time when the workers scrabble to get their share of the latest stock offering.

In the effort to woo back the Indians who leave as part of the massive brain drain, and re-invest in India, the government has instigated a special scheme. Indians abroad, whether they are Indian or foreign nationals (as long as their parents were born in India) have a special status of Non-resident Indian or NRI. They, their spouses and children enjoy all the privileges of an Indian national except voting rights. They are described as 'having Indian origins' which is particularly amusing if the spouse happens to be a white American or English.

English is the common language of business all over India and business cards printed in English are extensively used. Be sure to have all your qualifications clearly listed after your name. Qualifications in India are worn on the sleeve – certainly flaunted on a business card. You may recall the famous MA (Calcutta Failed). . .

TIME-KEEPING

If you have an official appointment make sure you turn up on time but be prepared to wait a long time. It is a standing joke that IST (Indian Standard Time) really stands for *Indian Stretchable Time*. If it is a social function then double-check with your hosts, although almost every one in India expects to turn up at least an hour late!

Indian women are to be increasingly found at every level in business, and there is no problem with businesswomen visiting India. However, travelling alone at night is not recommended. Women should also be aware, that inviting a male colleague to your hotel room for a business meeting is quite likely to be misunderstood by the local community and you will be treated accordingly.

No book on India would be complete without some mention of corruption. It has so come to pervade every strata in society that it is no longer considered corruption – just a fact of life. Everyone has a number two account. The word corruption does not mean anything anymore. 'Surcharge' or 'an Indian custom' might be a better description. Every contract can be fiddled, any privilege bought, every examination wangled. Businessmen regularly pay huge sums of money to ministers and bureaucrats if not to expedite some application form or the other then specifically not to obstruct it. The speed with which something is achieved has often been described as 'how big a smile you put on the face of the relevant bureaucrat or minister'. Here again, perhaps it is best to be guided by your business partner if you are planning to do business in India.

With 150,000 post offices, India has the largest postal network in the world; efficiency, however, is another matter. It can sometimes take two weeks for a letter to travel fifty kilometres. As letters going to foreign countries have to have *tikets* – stamps, quite 'expensive' by Indian standards, it is not unusual for the stamps to disappear from the envelopes and be reused. Stamped letters should be 'defaced' at the post office or better still, letters should be taken to a main post office where they will be franked for the right amount of money. There are plenty of international couriers for urgent letters in all the major cities.

CURRENCY

The Rupee is around fifty to the Pound Sterling and thirty to the Dollar. The visitor can be inundated by offers to change money on the black market. But since the convertibility of the Indian Rupee in 1992 there is very little premium and not worth anyone's while to take the risk.

It is illegal to take Indian currency out of the country, nor can you spend it in the duty-free shops. Any remaining rupees can be changed back at the airport as long as you have the original encashment receipt, this is valid for three months. It is worth keeping the encashment receipts as foreigners are expected to pay all hotel, air and rail invoices in foreign currency. Rupees are accepted provided they are accompanied by the encashment certificate to prove they have been purchased from an authorized dealer. Remember to keep Rs 300 airport tax, as it is payable prior to international departure.

The Rupee is made up of 100 *paisa*. One *lakh* is a hundred thousand and one *crore* is ten million.

8

Travelling in India

'The world's second biggest rail network'

AIR

The huge size of India means a heavy demand on local flights which often result in overbooking, delays and cancellation without notice. During winter months, particularly those flights originating from Delhi, are frequently subject to delay due to fog. To minimize inconvenience it is essential to reconfirm domestic and international flights and confirm departure times.

Luggage to go in the hold has to be scanned and security-tagged prior to check-in. You can expect further security checks on route to the aircraft and you will probably be required to identify your baggage again on the tarmac before it goes into the hold. Failure to identify the baggage will ensure that it will be left behind.

RAILWAYS

The world's largest civilian employer with 16 million workers, India has the world's second biggest rail network. Travelling by train is romantic and fun for short journeys such as Delhi-Agra or Bombay to Pune. If you have plenty of time and want to have a flavour of the country, then travelling by air-conditioned class or one of the special trains like 'Palace on Wheels' can be a pleasant experience. No Indian train travels fast, but at least the mail and express trains keep travelling most of the time unlike the passenger trains that stop at every town and city for long periods.

If you are sharing a compartment be vigilant about your luggage. The most popular item sold at railway stations is a chain and padlock – to ensure that during the night no one walks off with your suitcase whilst you are travelling.

ROAD

Car rental in India is unlike that in the West. There are very few self-drive companies, so you are limited to hiring a car and driver. This can be expensive for long periods because the cost of cars, fuel and upkeep is quite expensive in India even by Western standards.

The roads are shared with bullock carts, camels, goats and cows. It is quite important not to run over a cow. The cow may be sacred to the Hindus but everyone unites against the common enemy who might inadvertently run into a cow sleeping in the middle of the highway. Travelling at night between major cities which may be hundreds of miles apart is also not recommended as gangs of dacoits (robbers, from the word *daka* – to rob) are known to roam the countryside.

There are two types of taxi, usually the black-and-yellow ones operate within the state boundary and the tourist taxis, generally white, have an inter-state or all-India licence. It is important to check this before hiring one if you are planning an inter-state visit, otherwise you might be asked to pay a large amount of money at the border. It is also important to agree on a price before starting the journey as meters generally are either out of date or not switched on.

Most cities have motorized scooters, cycle rickshaws, the occasional horse-drawn carriage called a *tonga*, and of course buses and coaches. In some tourist and beach resorts you can also hire self-drive motorcycles and scooters if you do not place a very high value on your life!

'Traffic'

HEALTH REQUIREMENTS

No immunization is required but the more adventurous you are the more necessary it is to take precautions. It is wise, however, to make sure you have had your booster (required every 10 years) for tetanus. A travel insurance policy to cover theft, loss and medical problems is also a good idea.

Remember to include disposable needles for injections in case you ever require them in India. The 'disposable' needles available in pharmacies may have been resurrected from hospital waste bins and only been superficially cleaned.

Mosquitoes do not seem to bother the indigenous population but they are a problem in certain parts of India, and are the cause of malaria. The best way to avoid them is to stay in an air-conditioned hotel. All the chemists are well stocked with mosquito repellents like *Odomos* – a cream which applied to face, arms and other uncovered parts of the body is quite effective. For a bite-free night in the absence of a mosquito net or air-conditioning you could try *All Out* or *Good Night*. These are small vials of nerve gas, which are placed in a small electric container and keep the mosquitoes at bay when switched on. Costing less than Rs 200, they seem to be quite harmless to human beings for short periods.

For most of India, the best time to visit is between October and April. Nevertheless, it is considered a year-round destination because its geographical position, climatic conditions are widely diversified, on both a seasonal and regional basis.

9

The Language

India has something like 16 major languages and an estimated 874 regional dialects. The Dravidians with their group of seven major and many minor languages were already in southern India when the Aryans arrived with Sanskrit. The Dravidian languages are today spoken by over 110 million people.

In the 19th century English became the medium of higher education, the language of administration and the *lingua franca* among the educated population. Since the British left in 1947 it has been in competition with Hindi, the national language. Hindi is a mixture of words derived from Sanskrit and Urdu the court language left by the Persians and still used by the Muslims. It is written in the same script as Sanskrit which is Devanagari. The government had hoped that having a national language would produce a national identity – but the southern Indians do not understand it and generally rely on English to communicate with the northern Indian. Indeed, English is often referred to as the only language common to all Indians.

Indian English has acquired a special vocabulary which includes firstly, words from Indian languages commonly used in English-language publications in India. These may have mythological, philosophical or religious references: *Ram, Shiva, Yoga, Buddha* etc. Others are concerned with political activity: *bandh, hartal, Naxalite, Satyagraha*; sociology (*Harijan, Adivasi*); clothing (*jodhpurs, pajama, sari*); titles (*mahatma, pundit, sahib, sardar*); food (*vindaloo, curry, naan, dal*); and music (*sitar, tabla, sarangi*).

ANGLO-INDIAN VOCABULARY

Origins of some words that have found their way into the English language:

Bazaar	market
Calico	a cotton material, originally produced in Calicut, a town in south-western India.
Chintz	*chint* – a word meaning print
Chit	*chitti* – letter
Cooee	*koi* – anyone?
Cot	*khat* – a light bed
Cummerbund	*cummer* – waist, *bund* – close or to cover
Cushy	*khushi* – happy
Goolies	*Goli* – ball
Loot	from the word – to plunder
Mufti	*muft* – free, apparel worn during one's free time
Pajamas	*pai* – foot, *jama* – to enclose

Posh	Cabins situated **P**ort **O**ut **S**tarboard **H**ome – would ensure sight of the coastline whilst travelling on the steamers to India and back – and hence were more sought after.
Pukka	finished or well prepared.
Pakana	– to cook
Punch (as in drink)	the number five – *panch*. This was originally made with five ingredients and considered cooling – arrack (palm or coconut liquor), tea, sugar, lemon-juice and water.
Pundit	– priest/astrologer, now meaning wise head/commentator
Thug	from the word – to cheat

The advantage of mastering a few simple words and phrases means that you will be less vulnerable, as it will be assumed that you have spent a long time in India.

BASIC VOCABULARY

enough	*bas*
hot/cold	*garam/thanda*
chillie (hot)	*mirchie*
yes/no	*han/nahin*
please	*kripaya* or *mehaarbani se*
thank you	*dhanyabad* or *shukriya*
OK, good	*atcha*
genuine, cooked, ripe	*pukka*
bad	*kharab*
big/small	*bara/chotta*
American	*Amreekan*
English	*Angrez*
person, anyone	*wallah* – as in *chai* (tea) *wallah*
tip	*Baksheesh*

Did You Know?

India:
- is the world's largest democracy
- is the world's largest tea producer
- has the largest output of full-length feature films – over 700 annually since 1979
- has the second largest railway system and domestic airline
- is the third largest producer of milk and tobacco
- is the fourth largest producer of wheat, coal, nitrogenous fertilizers
- is the fifth largest producer of cement, cotton, potatoes
- is the sixth largest producer of iron ore
- is the seventh largest industrial economy
- is thirteen times the size of the United Kingdom
- its Himalayan range has 95 peaks above 7,500 metres high, the word 'Himalaya' means 'abode of snow'
- its Thar desert covers 260,000 square metres, almost twice the size of Bangla Desh
- has the wettest place on earth, Mawsynram – with 11,873 mm (467½ inches) in annual rainfall, ten times more than New York and 20 more than London
- has 450 million cows, that is one cow for every two people. As the cow is considered holy no one dares to kill them
- will have over a billion people by the year 2000, a baby is born every 1.2 seconds.

In test cricket the best all round record is held by Kapil Dev, who scored 5248 runs, 434 wickets and 64 catches in 131 matches.

Bombay duck is not duck at all, it is a kind of dried fish used in certain curries in Bombay.

Appendix

VISAS

Requirements for travel documents need to be checked prior to departure as these can often change. Everyone needs a visa for India. Tourist visas are normally valid for six months, not from the date of arrival in India but from the date of issue of the visa. If your stay in India is going to take you beyond 180 days of the date of issue you will have to set a few days aside to get it extended. Some official sources say it is free but charges of around Rs600 have been reported. Three-month extensions are routinely given and you will need four passport photographs. You will also require permits if you want to visit restricted areas like Sikkim. Both these are available from the Foreigner's Registration Offices.

SOME USEFUL ADDRESSES

Government of India, Tourist Offces:

88 Janpath, New Delhi: Tel: 320005/8

191 The Mall, Agra: Tel: 72377

123 M Karve Road, Bombay: Tel:293144/ 291585

4 Shakespeare Sarani, Calcutta: Tel: 441402/ 441475

154 Anna Salai, Madras: Tel: 88685/88686